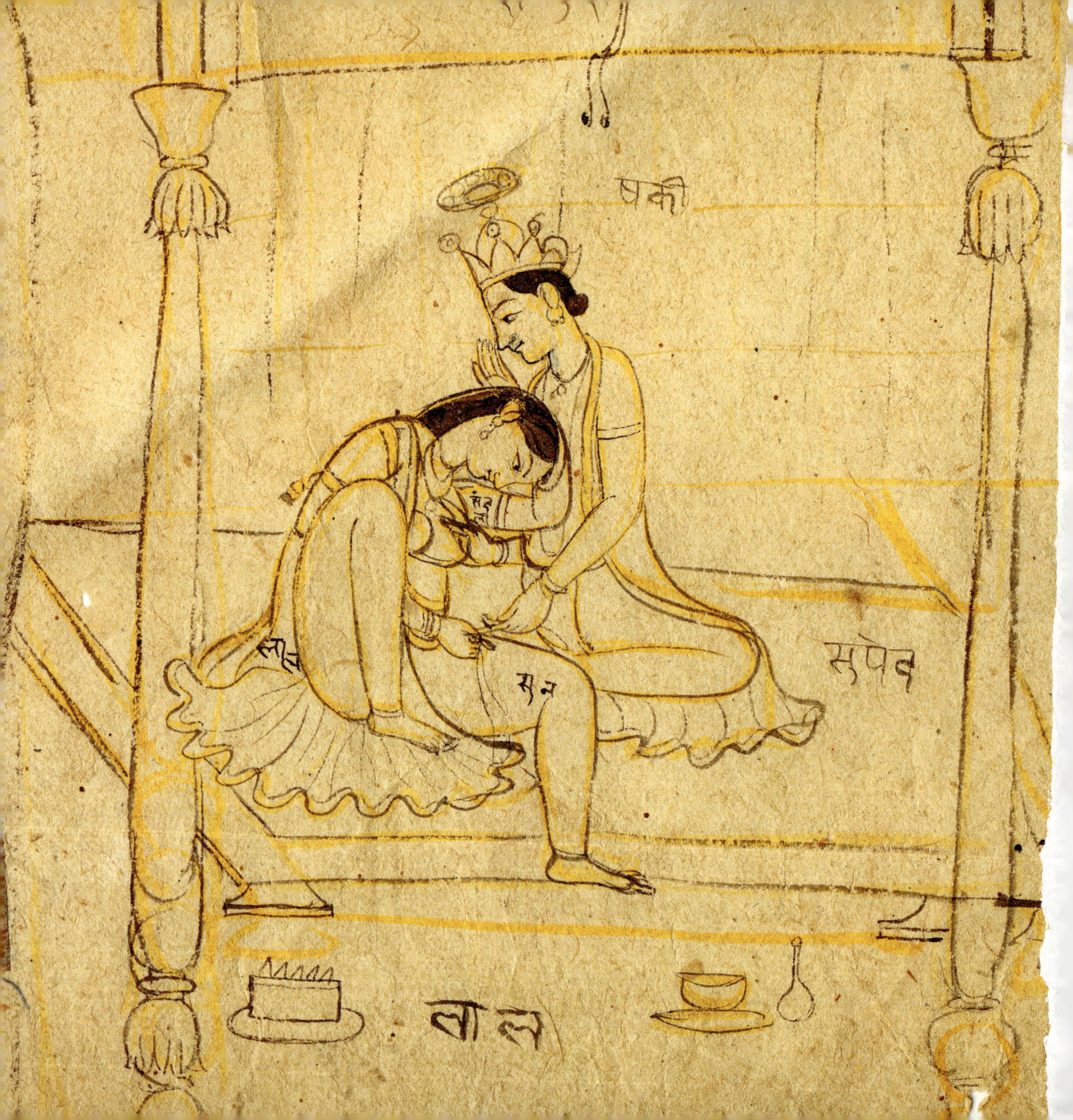

सुपेद
लाल

॥ कृष्ण दर्शन ॥

Glimpses of Krishna

Krishna as Poetry

॥ कृष्णः स्वयं काव्यम् ॥

Radha–Krishna, painting in Basohli style by Vijay Sharma

Krishna as Poetry

॥ कृष्णः स्वयं काव्यम् ॥

Conceived by
Harsha V. Dehejia

Paintings by
Vijay Sharma

DK PRINTWORLD
Publishers of Indian Traditions

Cataloging in Publication Data — DK
[Courtesy: D.K. Agencies (P) Ltd. <docinfo@dkagencies.com>]

Krishna as poetry = Kṛṣṇaḥ svayaṁ kāvyam / conceived by
Harsha V. Dehejia ; paintings by Vijay Sharma.
pages cm
Images copyright: Dehejia Collection of Krishna Art.
ISBN 9788124609675

1. Krishna (Hindu deity) — Poetry. 2. Krishna (Hindu deity) — Art.
3. Religious poetry, Indic — Translations into English. 4. Miniature painting, Indic. I. Dehejia, Harsha V., editor. II. Sharma, Vijay, 1962- artist. III. Dehejia Collection of Krishna Art. IV. Title: Kṛṣṇaḥ svayaṁ kāvyam.

LCC BL1220.K75 2019 | DDC 294.52113 23

ISBN: 978-81-246-0967-5

First published in India, 2019

Printed and published by:
D.K. Printworld (P) Ltd.
Regd. office: "Vedaśrī", F-395, Sudarshan Park
New Delhi - 110 015
Phones : (011) 2545 3975, 2546 6019
e-mail : indology@dkprintworld.com
Web : www.dkprintworld.com

Artists: Padma Shri Vijay Sharma, Parikshit Sharma, Trilok Soni, Girish Patel, Women Embroiderers of Chamba

Designed by: Shrinidhi Sridhar, Ottawa, Canada,

Font used: Garamond, Remachine

Calligraphy: Ram Kasture

Sanskrit words are italicized without diacritical marks.

नाहम वसामि वैकुंठे योगिनाम् हृदय नच ।
मद् भक्ता यत्र गायन्ति तत्र तिष्ठामि नारद ॥

I dwell not in Vaikuntha, nor in the hearts of *yogi*s.
Where my devotees sing, there be I, Oh Narada!
– *Padma Purana*

A poet venerate a nayika, painting by Vijay Sharma in Kangra style

कृष्ण एक काव्य

Krishna, a Poem

Once, all the gods gathered in heaven and they were in an animated conversation. There was Shiva on His Nandi with a *trishula* in His hand, and Parvati by His side; Vishnu sat in all His glory holding the *padma*, *chakra*, *shankha* and *gada*; Devi came charging sitting on Her tiger wielding Her trident and crushing Mahisha and there was Brahma with his four heads and holding the Veda and He presided over the assembly. There were also minor gods like Kama, Kubera, Agni and Marut, and many *ganas* and demi-gods. Each god started describing his own prowess and his function in *samsara* and each felt he was the greatest of them all. Just then a beautiful woman, looking like an *apsaras*, walked in, with dancing steps, she had a neck like that of a swan and thighs like the plantain plant, her breasts were like jars and her lips that of the *bimba* fruit.

The gods looked at her with amazement and asked, "Who are you?" Coyly she said , "I am Kavita." "And what is that?" the gods asked.

Kavita said, "I am *shruti* the primal voice."

"And how is Kavita born?" Brahma asked, since he was the creator god.

Kavita said, "Kavita is the *shruti* and is the *adi* and the *anadi*, it is the primal cosmic *vani*, *anhad*, unborn and undying, heard in the deepest recesses of the mind of the *kavi*, who then transforms it into words. The *kavi* then enriches the words with *rasa*, ornaments with *alamkara*, adds *chanda* and *tala*, makes them *ramaniya* and then *kavita* is transformed from *shruti* into *kavya* and thus it is that the *kavi* is also a creator."

The gods were amazed and they all wanted Kavita to be with them, but Kavita refused and the gods felt hurt. "I belong to the heart and not to the mind, I live in streams of *rasa* and not in rivers of *karma*, my home is in the assembly of poets and not in the commerce of the market, I am the cause of *ananda* and not of *sukha*, I am knowledge and not just pleasure," she said.

Just then she heard the notes of the flute and she began to follow it. The mellifluous sound led her to the Kadamba tree where Krishna *muralidhara* was standing underneath it, playing the flute. She bowed to Him and then merged into Him and gave up her individual existence but lived within Krishna, the *sakar* who became *nirakar*.

Brahma got up from his seat in heaven and came down to earth and pointing to Krishna said that now Kavita abides in you and therefore:

krishnah svayam kavyam।

Krishna is Himself Poetry.

The gods applauded, and said Krishna is the *kavi* and the *kavya*. The minor gods moved in their aerial chariots, the sun and the moon appeared and the galaxy shone with a thousand stars.

Just then Sarasvati also came to earth and asked, "how will Kavita be expressed for the *nirakar* needs an *akar*, a subject needs to be transformed into an object?" Narada interjected and asked, "why should Kavita be expressed, she lives within Krishna?" Sarasvati said, "Within Krishna she is *nirakar*, *nihshabda*, *nirvachana*, *nirkaya*. Surely she must be expressed for the *nirakar* wishes to become *sakar*, the *nihshabda* wants to express itself in words, *purusha* wants to be involved with *prakriti*. This is the *dharma* of everything that lives." The voice of Kavita within Krishna agreed for did not Sarasvati herself produce a son, Kavyapurusha, who spoke the first *kavya*. But yet, language Kavita said, is not *purna*, it reveals only a quarter while three quarters remain hidden in a cave. Further, words must be written only then *kavya* gets established. Then came Bharatamuni and said, "Kavita should be expressed through dance for that is the perfect art form". This had no effect on Kavita as dance she said is ephemeral.

Vishvakarma, the divine architect, came and insisted that Kavita be represented through *shilpa* (sculpture), yet Kavita was unmoved. For she felt that *shabda*, *natya* and *shilpa* could not do justice to her beauty and her tender feelings of love. Finally Vishnu descended to earth and painted an image of Urvashi on his thighs. Kavita was impressed and said, "let me be expressed through painting, for a painting is the best representation of feelings and what is more, it adds colours to those sentiments. And thus paintings of Krishna's *leela*s and *krida*s were born, full of colour and texture, where there were birds and blossoms, the peacock and the *koyal*, where the Yamuna flowed and in its waves were the sounds of *ghungharu* and above all one heard in the paintings the sweet sound of the flute. When Krishna *kavya* like the *Bhagavata Purana* and the *Gita Govinda* became popular, illustrated manuscripts of these *kavya*s were produced in courtly ateliers and *kavya* had a visual and an aural life. Kavita was pleased and she inspired poets and painters for 500 years to create beautiful Krishna poetry of His love and joy, of His dance and delight, of His *leela*s and *krida*s, poetry and books that were both *shravya* and *drishya kavya*.

All the gods in heaven blessed Krishna, flowers rained from the sky, the light of the sun showed Krishna the paths of Vrindavana and the light of the moon illumined the *nikunja*s in the enchanted forest, pairs of birds on the Kadamba tree sang Raga Megha Malhar and as clouds in the sky turned *ghanashyama*, the peacocks danced to the rhythm of Vasanta Raga and the entire world around Krishna became *krishnamaya*. There was an *akashvani*:

krishnah svayam kavyam

It is said that Krishna's *shringara leela*s are expressed in poetry but this is only a half truth, for Krishna is *svayam kavyam* and the *adi shringara kavi* and those who are touched by Krishna's Shringara Rasa become *krishnamaya* that is the ultimate truth. Therefore, we say that *krishna svayam kavyam*.

Thus, Krishna manifests Himself through *kavya* and *kavya* seeks the *kavi* even as the *kavi* inspires the *rasika* and the *rasika* reaches Krishna. This is the *aroha* and *avaroha* of Krishna *kavya*.

Just then there was a voice from a *kavi* who said:

God in many religious traditions is considered the creator of this universe. The Hindu tradition on the other hand strikes a different note in the Nasadiya Sukta when it declares, "We do not know who created the universe, even the gods do not know". The Nataraja or the Cosmic Shiva, it is said, brings the creation into being with the drum and His dancing feet. Those of us steeped in the mellifluous love of Krishna feel that it is He who created this universe through His heart-throbbing poetry and thus we say Krishna is the *adi kavi* and the very earth, its sounds and songs, its colours and movements, and everything that is touched by His *shringara*, is His poetry.

Has it not been said, *kavya ham rati kavyam*?

It is said that poets are born and not created for every poet is a product of a certain environment that creates and shapes his mind. That aesthetic environment is made up of the spaces within the mind and the rhythms of the outside world. In that poetic mind reside *samskara*s (latent psychic impressions) from a previous birth; it has thoughts and ideas; it experiences dreams and emotions and is influenced by the many events of a lived life. That mind is chastened with various myths and metaphors, with stories heard in village squares and in the *chowk* of one's home. That beautiful mind resonates with stories from street theatre and from the chatter of friends and family. And above all it has a rich storehouse of the poetry of the past that has flowed down like a river and which nourishes the mind. From all this arise poetic creations.

The sounds of a bubbling brook and the mute grandeur of the Himalayas, the playful waves of the ocean, the dark clouds in the sky heralding the rain, the serenity of an azure lake, the highways that lead to the cloud-kissing mansions and the footfalls that take us to the peace of a hermitage, the dance of the peacock and the song of the *koyal*, the colours of the Champa and the winding vine around the trunk of a tree are all expressions of His poetry, nay of Krishna Himself.

The innumerable shining stars in the vast and boundless sky are the words of His poem and the *hum* that comes from the depths of the earth is the *atman* of that poem. The chirping of the birds is the voice of the poem. The title page of the poem is the sun that arises from the womb of dawn. And the images on the front page of this cosmic poem are the beautiful white flowers of the Parijata that blooms in the morning and creates a carpet on the earth; the shining drops of dew on the blades of grass and the rivulets flowing like streams of milk are its lyrics.

With every new morning the title page of the book of poetry changes. Krishna once more writes the heading of the book with the first rays of the sun and as the day progresses the world of nature reads this book and as darkness descends it rests in the pages of the blackness of the night. With the advent of another morning the lines of the poetry start appearing all over again, the title page forms one more time, the headings are written afresh and nature starts reading this book of poems anew and Krishna stands before us in all His glory as the primal poet.

Krishna as the creator of this cosmic poetry is also the primal witness of His creation. He is both the *kavi* and the *kavya* at the same time. His creations are timeless as they defy time. When it comes to Krishna on the road of time history spreads itself like a sheet, and on this path evolves the journey of human beings with measured movements and Krishna plants the seed of love in the human heart and says to live is to love and to love is to know.

Who then is a poet and what is his *dharma*? Who is the poet who creates beautiful *kavya* in the Vedas we do not know, but we do know that he is a true artist and creates pictures and not narratives through his words, pictures that speak of the collective awe and wonder at the world around. The Vedic poet holds an exalted position, he is called a *prajapati* (leader of the people) who can give a name to each ray of the rising sun. And through trackless generations we in India have honoured the poet and held him in great esteem. He sculpts and ornaments words, makes sure that one word relates to the next in a bond of friendship and infuses them with *rasa* so that even a single sentence enriched with *rasa* is poetry. The poet uncovers what we sometimes fail to see, he reveals hidden connections, suggests rather than points and paints another more beautiful reality which brings us close to the mystery of the oneness of the universe and the human condition and ultimately leads us to the poetic truth. This truth need not be historic or rational yet it creates ripples of pleasure (*ananda*). Ghanananda puts it beautifully when he writes, "others may call me a poet but my writing of poetry is only an excuse for remembering Krishna and Radha".

A poet venerates Krishna, painting by Vijay Sharma in Mewar style

And what if the poet is none other than Krishna? His form is verily poetry, His *tribhanga* stance captures the dance of the universe, His movements are the lyrics of a love song, the sound of His flute is the mellifluous melody of the *prana* of the universe and a call to eternity, His colour *ghanashyama* takes us from the rhythms of the earth to the clouds of Ashadha, His crown of peacock feather is the dance of nature and the *vanamala* exudes the fragrance of love and He ensures that by His very *sannidhya* (presence) He spreads love everywhere.

The poet that creates Krishna *kavya* is no different for he is wonderstruck by Krishna, the many colours and sounds, fragrance and movements from His mere presence: the yellow of His *pitambara* and the *ghanashyama* of His body which take us from the earth to the sky, the multicoloured flowers of His *vanamala* from which arises the fragrance of life, the blue of His peacock feather which is the joyous dance of rain, the mellifluous notes of His flute and the music of the *nupura* from His dancing feet. Just as the Vedic *rishi*s heard the *shruti* which became the Vedic hymns, Krishna poetry is heard in the recesses of the mind of the poet, it is the *anhad* Krishna *nada*, devoid of words. Where the mere resonance of the formless Krishna *nada* is transformed into the form of *kavya*. That *kavya* is not a narrative but fragments of romantic moments so beautiful that it contains the whole universe of feelings within it and connects us all in His embrace.

Our wisdom tradition thus starts on a poetic note, our *mantra*s are to be chanted, our sacred speech is to be sung, Sarasvati holds a *vina* and Shiva is the cosmic dancer with a *damaru* in hand. With music and dance what is *shravya* (spoken) becomes *drishya* (visible), *nada* (sound) is *geya* (sung), *chhanda* (metre) becomes *tala* (rhythm) and thus is dance created. Poetry, therefore, is multidimensional and synaesthetic. Thus for us, beautiful thought or truth, sacred or secular, assumes many different poetic forms, rather than being a commandment, and in doing so it endears itself to us. As Mammata said poetry "is as if a loving wife talks to us and not a teacher who instructs us". For almost a thousand years our sacred thought appeared as a forest dialogue and later as a Puranic narrative, and it was not until the *Bhagavata Purana* of the ninth century that we return once again to poetry and Krishna appears as a *kavi*, his *leela*s and *krida*s become *kavyamaya* and his romantic persona becomes *kavya*. The arid intellectual debates about the nature of Ultimate Reality which characterized the first millennium of our wisdom traditions was replaced by the songs of Krishna in the second millennium that whispered poetic truth. Thus it is that we say that *krishnah svayam kavyam*. Krishna creates pictures of *shringara*, not a narrative; He creates fragments of romantic moments in which there is a whole universe of feelings, He shows fleeting moments of sensuality which are reminders of His spirituality, there is poetry in His pictures and pictures in His poetry and it is because of this that His *madhurya* is *jnana*.

Radha–Krishna frolicking, Bundi, 17th century, Ramesh Kapoor collection

The romantic Krishna is celebrated in a variety of arts and crafts and not so much in doctrine or ritual. Poetry and song, dance and drama, *sanjhi* and *rangoli*, embroidery and mural and above all painting are the many ways in which artists and artisans participate in the *leela*s and *krida*s of Krishna and convert it into visual poetry. So inviting are the romantic sports of Krishna that they lend themselves to many artistic representations.

The *Bhagavata Purana* was a turning point not only in the understanding of Krishna but equally of Indian thought. Until this point Krishna was the central figure of the

Mahabharata and then the charioteer of Arjuna. Religion, if one can use that word for the Hindu tradition, was based on right and ethical conduct. Arjuna was a person in existential despair. However, in the *Srimad Bhagavatam*, Krishna no longer needs to give a sermon but He is a cowherd who engages with the *gopa*s and *gopi*s of Vrindavana with the sports and songs of love, apparently for pleasure, but mainly to impart knowledge as well, through *shringara*. Krishna seems to say that to live is to love and to love is to know. Once He assumes *shringara rupa*, the love of Krishna was expressed in words and lyric, in song and dance, in painting and on murals, by classical and folk artists, in homes and *haveli*s, by court artists and ordinary women for a thousand years and continues even today. Many are its expressions, varied in forms, whether on paper or fabric, on mud walls or temple sculptures, even if it is sung in *raga*s (folk melodies). However the *pratibha* (the inspiration) for all of this comes from the *sahitya* of Krishna poetry, and when this poetry is deeply felt, Krishna does not remain a distant deity or a god to be worshipped by rites and rituals but becomes *kavya* (poetry) itself, to be celebrated aesthetically.

Whether He is Govinda or Mohan, Madhava or Madhukara, Giridhari or Nandakumara, Shyam or Ghanashyam, Natavara or Damodara, Yogeshvara or Raseshvara, when all His names are understood, when His flute is heard in the inner spaces of the mind, when He colours our mind with the *neel* of His limbs or the *pitambara* of His clothes, when the colours of the paintings colour our mind or when our heart beats in unison with His dancing steps, our entire being feels Him, neither as God nor as an *avatara*, but as the living embodiment of *shringara kavya*, for of the various *rasa*s, it is *shringara* where Krishna resides. It is through Krishna poetry that we become *rasamaya*, through the sound of His *bansuri* that we become *nadamaya*, through His rhythms in the *rasa* that we become *talamaya* and through the *dhvani* of His *shringara* that we become *kavyamaya*, and when all these come together we become *anandamaya*. All of this through the aesthetic celebration of Krishna *shringara* through poetry and its transformation in the various arts.

The *Bhagavata Purana*, the central text of the Vaishnavas, enunciates in a simple narrative and poetic form, through

Bikaner, 18th century,
Dehejia Collection of Krishna Art

Dvaitavada the romantic relationship and the amorous dalliance of Krishna and the *gopi*s, a love that is located in the enchanted forest of Vrindavana. Couched in the language, the motifs and the metaphors of *shringara*, the *Rasa Panchadhyayi* of the *dashama skandha* of the *Bhagavata* (X.29-33), while presenting some tender and lyrical moments of the love of Krishna and the *gopi*s, celebrates initially the beautiful *dvaita* of love, with its sweet delights of amorous pleasures, and then almost surreptitiously leads us to the door of *advaita* of that very love. All of this interplay happens within the joyous matrix of Shringara Rasa and its beautifully romantic moments in poetry and painting and not through arid intellectuality, a world denying *maya* or ascetic or religious rites and rituals. There is in the *Bhagavata* no negation or any sense of unreality, only a joyous sensual and emotional affirmation and then moving that reality to another level, not the Vedantic *neti neti*, but a beautiful *iti iti*.

Romantic love is in and of this world, it must necessarily be sensuous and this worldly, and Krishna as the *gopi*s know Him in the *dashama skandha* is entirely human and not divine, and therefore a source of sensual pleasures. For as the *gopi*s say:

> *krishnam viduh param kantam na tu brahmataya mune*।
>
> We know Krishna as our beloved and not as divinity.
>
> – *Bhagavata* X.29.12

The *Bhagavata* posits Krishna as the paragon of sweetness and hence gives him epithets such as *madhukara* or *madhupati*. Krishna exudes *madhurya* through His acts and His gestures, His words and His flute, His clothes and His sports, in fact Krishna is nothing but a *madhura kavya*. Loving tenderness, lyrical softness, delicate movements, fragrant limbs, the mellifluous sounds of His flute, His innocent pranks, evocative clothes, beautiful adornments such as the *vanamala*, serene sensuality, graceful manners, charming and sensitive, passionate but not lustful, demanding but not aggressive, all add up to the *madhurya* of Krishna, a *madhurya* that defines His love, and which He richly shares with the *gopi*s of Vrindavana and which is a beautiful poetry. And the idyllic and sensuous Vrindavana provides the perfect setting for the sweet love of Krishna. It is here where the lyrical Yamuna flows, clouds shower rain as if they were flowers, peacocks dance in ecstasy, birds sing passionately, blossoms bloom affectionately and whisper words of love, winding creepers caress the trunks of trees as if a *premika* embraces her beloved, fruit-laden branches bend to provide a blessing with a sylvan canopy, bees dance around lotus pollen and sing a love song, cranes and swans fly towards and cows are drawn to the call of the flute and fragrant sandalwood winds intoxicate the mind, and thus it is that Vrindavana becomes the perfect landscape in which *madhurya* unfolds and all around there are flowing streams of honey as if to fully reveal Vishnu in themselves. Isn't this poetry? The *Bhagavata* makes this firm connection between the joys and abundance of spring, its songs and its rhythms and the indwelling Vishnu, a Vishnu that resides not only in the minds and hearts of the *gopi*s but also in the sap that animates the birds and the bees, the trees and the creepers of Vrindavana, for to express joy and dance to the rhythms of Vasanta, as in a Vasanta Ragini, is to fully express Vishnu and realize Krishna. As the *Bhagavata* X.35.9 says:

> *vanalatastarava atmani vishnum vyanjayantya iva pushpaphaladhayah*।

Krishna as Vishnu, according to the *Bhagavata*, is not to be expressed by knowledge or devotion or through ascetic rites and religious rituals, neither by inward contemplation and life-negating attitudes, but by ecstatic and evocative expressions of love that affirm one's own sensuality and that of everything around. This is the hallmark of Krishna poetry. The *Bhagavata* describes him as a *natavaravapuh*, one who is charming as an accomplished actor, in the following lines:

Cut out from Manku's *Bhagavata Purana*, Mankot, 19th century, private collection

> Possessed of a charming personality like an accomplished actor graced with a crown of peacock feathers his ears decorated with Karnikara flowers clad in brilliant garments yellow like molten gold wearing the Vaijayanti garland made of five different flowers filling the holes of his flute with the nectar of his lips and accompanied by cowherds singing of his glory Krishna entered Vrindavana which was beautified by his foot prints. – 21.5

> Krishna wore a crest of peacock feathers and appeared as a forest dweller with Karnikara flowers adorning his ears. He rested his face on his left arm breathing through the flute with appropriate movements of his eyebrows and fingers. He made the cowherds sing from the Gandharva Veda and gave delight to all creatures of the world. – 21.6

> Picturesquely clad in garments intertwined with tender mango leaves with tufts of peacock feathers and bunches of flowers and wearing garlands of lilies and lotuses and singing and dancing freely in the midst of cowherds Krishna and Balarama looked exceedingly beautiful like actors on the stage. – 21.8

The various adornments of Krishna are a paradigm of the joys of mellifluous spring, the yellow of mango blossoms and the swarm of honey bees, the festive beauty of the earth that is in bloom, of verdant nature in love with everything around, of perfumed winds that intoxicate lovers and of peacocks dancing at the sight of the blue-black rain clouds of Ashadha and the notes of His flute are a whisper of His *prana* (life breath) and the essence of His very being. And the call of that flute is His invitation and evocation to discover and realize our own *atman* and the indwelling *madhura dhara* (streams of honey) within ourselves. Krishna's adornments are thus not just decorations, they are an *atmadarshana* (visual knowledge of our own *atman*), our true and ultimate selves and it is in this sense that He is both a *kavi* and *kavya*.

Rasaleela, Nathadwara, 18th century, Dehejia Collection of Krishna Art

A central event in the *Bhagavata* is the *maharasa* on the full-moon night of Sharada. There are many ways in which we look at the *rasaleela* but according to Vaishnava doctrine the timeless and endless *rasaleela* of Krishna is the source of a stream of *rasa* that flows perpetually from the eternal Vrindavana to the earth and further it is this same *rasa* that flows as a stream of *rasa* to and between mankind. This is an aesthetic interpretation of this dance. It is a timeless dance in which the divine and the human lose themselves in the rhythms, movements and melodies of pure love just as we lose ourselves in the *ananda* of *kavya*. It is only fitting that the *rasaleela* has been called *sarva leela chudamani* (the crest jewel of all *leela*s of Krishna). The *rasaleela* is a river and a fountain which has no beginning and no end, it is a stream so broad that it has no other shore, it is an ocean of nectar and of youth, of life and vitality, of joy and bliss, to drink its waters is to find love and to be touched by its waters is to find freedom, to be blessed by it is to find divinity and to be nourished by is to find oneself, for has it not been said *rasa iva saha*. The *rasa* indeed is a *kavya* of nectar.

Krishna's *rasaleela* can be considered, ultimately, to be a *leela* of Krishna with Himself, *sva-pratibimba vibhramah* (playing with His own reflection). In other words Krishna is Himself a *kavi* and also a *rasika*. The *jiva* and the *gopi*s are a part of Krishna and Krishna was able to be with sixteen thousand *gopi*s at once because of the power of His *svarupa* to be manifest in an infinite number of forms without any effect on His true nature. The *rasaleela* is ultimately about stillness and not about movement, for even though Krishna multiplies and takes part in the circular dance holding hands with *gopi*s on both sides, He also stands at the still centre of the *rasa*; that is the source of energy, it is that unmoving centre which makes movement possible and into which all movement must end. It is when Krishna leaves and the *mandala* is dissolved that movement leads to stillness, *shringara* to *shringara bhakti*, a group activity becomes a personal search for the ultimate meaning of love. It is Krishna's flute that ensures that the *rasa* takes place outside time and beyond space, in a time which is beyond time and in a space that converts the earthly *gokula* to the celestial *goloka*.

However, the enchanted *dvaita* of Vrindavana while pleasing to the senses is a stepping stone to the serene grandeur of *advaita* as the pleasures of belonging must ultimately give way to the higher truth of longing. For when at the end of the *rasaleela* Krishna leaves Vrindavana never to return, the *gopi*s are heartbroken and look for Krishna, they wait and they search, they long and they seek the absent Krishna, but never do they stop loving Krishna. Love in longing in the case of the *gopi*s is even more intense than love in belonging, the heart throb of *viyoga* of the *gopi*s is more pulsating than the thrill of *samyoga*. But it is this poignant *viraha* that transforms the *gopi*s, chastens their minds and leads them towards a glorious and majestic *advaita*. The *gopi*s in their *viyoga* are not jilted but chastened, not angry but ready to take their love to a higher level, to transform *shringara* to *shringara bhakti*, and move the sensuous *dvaita* to a spiritual *advaita* as they see Krishna everywhere and all of Vrindavana becomes *krishnamaya*. Uddhava's sermon to the *gopi*s was like the buzzing of bees to the *gopi*s (*bhrahmara geet*) and it becomes clear through the simple lyrics of *bhrahmara geet* that the *gopi*s have internalized Krishna and that through their love they have achieved a spiritual union with Him even in the face of separation. Krishna poetry has moved from the *sthula* and the *sukshma* to the *para*, there is here a wholeness even when there is apparent fragmentation, an *advaita* that has arisen through the fires of *viraha*. There may be for the *gopi*s a physical *viyoga* but a spiritual *samyoga*, such is the strength and depth, the veracity and sincerity of their love. This is *shringara* at its best and this is *shuddha advaita* at work. This *advaita* of the *Bhagavata* has neither the negation of Shankara's Mayavada nor the theology of Ramanuja's Vishishtadvaita. It rests entirely on the sensuality of romantic love and its ability to chasten and transform the mind of the *gopi*s through the process of longing. And when there is this intimacy

of Krishna through love, there is no need for either contemplation or devotion that is generally reserved for God realization.

Bypassing Jayadeva, let us look at Bilvamangala, the itinerant singer from the south whose songs in praise of the child Krishna were compiled in two manuscripts: the *Krishnakarnamritam* and the *Balagopalastuti*. Bilvamangala locates the child Krishna in Vrindavana both as an object of veneration and wonder as he sings about the various *krida*s of the infant Krishna. Although the Krishna of Bilvamangala is basically that of the *Bhagavata*, there is a significant difference. In the *Balagopalastuti* we have a historical poet who upholds the child Krishna and who in his ecstatic vision sees the frolicking Krishna and like the lines of a poem derives *ananda* from His evocative sensuality. Note:

> Oh Lord! Even to this very day thousands of Upanishadic sages
> have not seen you with their eyes or in their hearts.
> Sweet is his face and his smile and is like the fragrance of honey
> with fresh *kumkuma* over his body . . . he steals the lotus of my heart
> whose jewelled anklets tinkle
> whose footprints adorn the paths of Vraja
> He has melted the hearts of the sages with the sound of his flute
> whose sweet form gives pleasure to the mind and eyes.

For Bilvamangala, Krishna is like a melodious song or a beautiful picture.

So popular were the songs of Bilvamangala that they spread to many parts of India and influenced even Vallabhacharya the founder of the Pushtimarga of Nathadwara. Mahaprabhu Vallabhacharya (1479–1531) established the Pushtimarga Sampradaya centred around Krishna as Shrinathji. While Surdas came into the fold even during Vallabhacharya's time it was his son Vitthalnath who created the many aesthetic expressions of Shrinathji at Nathadwara. Chief among this were the *ashtachhaapa kavi*s who sang about and to Krishna the many beautiful moments of Krishna's *shringara*.

Vallabhacharya's *Madhurashtakam* is a landmark in *Bhagavata kavya* for with the term *madhurya* he established both the epistemology and ontology of Krishna *shringara*. In other words, for Vallabhacharya, Krishna was both *kavi* and *kavya*. Not only every act and gesture, word and song, movement and dance of Krishna is *madhura* but Krishna by his very presence makes the entire Vrindavana *akhilam madhuram*. Krishna's *shringara* is no longer limited to the *gopi*s but like the *purnaghata* it overflows and envelops everyone around. The objective *madhura* becomes the subjective *madhurya* because of Krishna. And when there is this intimacy of Krishna through love, then there is no need for either contemplation or devotion that is generally reserved for God realization as Vallabha says in his *Subodhini*:

jnana bhaktyostu avirbhavartham upayogah।
– *Bhagavata* 29.15

Vallabhacharya inducted the *ashtachhaapa kavi*s of Nathadwara, chief of whom was Surdas who sings of the sensual charm of Krishna, as:

His tangled hair like honey-drinking bees
his eyebrows lovely playful fish
his crown and earrings, sun and sunbeams
murali's sound, the buzz of bees entranced
his teeth like light near a rain-bearing cloud.

and

When Hari appeared, I could only stare.
He is a sapphire daubed in sandal.
Every aspect of his body from head to toe
becomes a thief to your heart.,
like a woman captured in art.

Sursagar , Mewar, 18th century, National Gallery, Ottawa, Canada

Surdas picks up on the *bhramara geet* in the *Bhagavata* and writes lovingly of Uddhava's visit to Vrindavana and it is here in the simple but heart-throbbing lyrics that the *advaita* of the *Bhagavata* unfolds. The *gopi*s compare the words of Uddhava to the buzzing of bees. How, the *gopi*s ask, can even Krishna not know that He has stolen their minds when He left, *madhukara shyama hamare chor*, and therefore their love is always with Krishna, that their minds are *krishnamaya*, full of Krishna at all times and for them everything around them is nothing but Krishna.

It becomes clear through the simple lyrics of *bhramara geet* that the *gopi*s have internalized Krishna and that through their love they have achieved a spiritual union with Him even in the face of separation, Krishna poetry has moved from the *sthula* and the *sukshma* to the *para*, there is here a wholeness even when there is apparent fragmentation, an *advaita* that has arisen through the fires of *viraha* and *dvaita*. There may be for the *gopi*s a physical *viyoga* but there is a spiritual *samyoga*, such is the strength and depth, the veracity and sincerity of their love. This is *shringara* at its best and this is *shuddha advaita* at work. This *advaita* of the *Bhagavata* has neither the negation of Shankara's Mayavada nor the theology of Ramanuja's Vishishtadvaita. It rests entirely on the sensuality of romantic love and its ability to chasten and transform the mind of the *gopi*s through the process of longing.

The Advaitic mind of the *gopi*s having celebrated particularity in their romantic dalliance with Krishna now sees universality in the divinity of Krishna, it rejoices in unity where it once saw divisions, it delights in *purnatva* where it once divided the world into *aham* and *idam*, it rests in a serene silence where it once enjoyed the sounds of words or the colours of poetry, it experiences the mute touch of love when it once felt the thrill of a romantic embrace, it is that state of mind which says I am you and moves away from the concept of I and you, it is a mind which experiences beauty (*saundarya*) when it once beheld and affirmed the beautiful (*sundara*), it sees oneness when once it was mired in the dualities of pleasure and pain, life and death, *samyoga* and *viyoga*.

The changing of the seasons brings out Krishna in the soft light of Vasanta. Of the six seasons it is Vasanta (spring) that brings Krishna's *shringara* alive by the colours and sounds, the textures and the aromas, the mood and the ethos of the world of nature. Vasanta is *rituraja* (the king of seasons). It is in Vasanta that nature comes to life, mango blossoms appear, colours deepen, the birds and the bees are joyous, love awakens and erotic feelings quicken, the mind is energized and the heart throbs with excitement. Nature's fecundity and luxuriance are matched only by the heart-throbbing anticipation, amorous desires, tremulous coyness and expectant longing of the romantic *nayika*. In the various colours of the fecundity of Vasanta there is nature's romance, there is an *agamana* (a welcome), in its radiance there is an invitation, in its unspoken words there is a song of love, in its movements there is the dance of amour and in its quivering there is the tremulous desire of love. Nature in Vasanta is like a bride adorned in red like the *kinshuka* flower, *raktanshuka navavadhuhu eva*, in the words of Kalidasa (*Ritusamhara* 6.19). Vasanta is when the words of poetry dance and sing in Raga Basant.

**Raga Megha Mallhar Bundi,
18th century, Museum of Fine Art, Boston**

Kalidasa goes on to describe spring with these words:

Everything gains added beauty in spring, trees put forth flowers,
lotuses emerge from the waters,
ladies become passionate, the winds are fragrant,
evenings are pleasant and days are delightful. – 6.2

Karnikara and Ashoka blossoms adorn the ears of women
and *navamallika* their black and wavy hair. – 6.5

The cuckoo intoxicated with the liquor
of the juice of mango blossoms
kisses his mate passionately
while the humming bee dallies with its mate.
– 6.14

> The vernal season has covered the entire landscape with Kinshuka groves which are bent with blossoms and flutter in the wind and resemble a blazing fire while the earth appears like a newly-wedded wife with red garments. – 6.19

To be adorned is to invite and to welcome, to be bejewelled is to signal that the moment is right for the pleasures of love and in the desire to be beautiful there is the promise that nothing is more important to the *nayika* than the loving admiration and attention of her beloved. This is the rite of spring for mankind and nature alike. It is for this moment that she has waited and prepared with longing and anticipation. Yet there is a certain anxiety and apprehension, but in this very state of nervous animation there is a dedication and a commitment to the celebration of her love. It is clear that the beautiful expressions of Vasanta, and equally the adornment of the *nayika*, is not mere beautification but it is a rite and a ritual, a promise and a sacrament of love; for adornment is the bond that ties the beautiful to the beloved, the *nayika* to the *nayaka*, the verdant *prakriti* to the cosmic *Purusha*, man to God, asserting that the beautiful and beauty are an integral part not only of romantic love but of the sensually charged mind that luxuriates in Vasanta.

Jayadeva describes Vasanta in these words:

when the tender Malayan wind touches
the lovely clove creeper
when the grove is filled with the sound
of the cuckoo
intermingled with the sounds of
swarms of honey-making bees
Hari plays in the amorous spring time. – 1.28

If poetry is the dance of words, Krishna is *nateshvara* (the lord of dance), Himself. In the groves of Vrindavana and on the banks of the Yamuna, Krishna plays amorously and spreads His love through dance. There is in the beauty of the dancing body of Krishna not only motion but a certain meaning, not just action but a pulsating emotion, and not the mere ability to negotiate the commerce of life but to rise above the banal and the pedantic and to express the celestial and the transcendent. When Krishna dances the world around Him dances, His movements resonate

with the rhythms of the earth and His flute provides the melody to the song of the birds and blossoms. Unlike Shiva as Nataraja who dances for Himself, Krishna dances for the *gopi*s, He dances so that others can dance with Him and experience through the dance His love, and just as the dancing words of *kavya* touch the *rasika*, Krishna's dance of joy and love reverberates in all of Vrindavana so that *gopi*s and *gopa*s, birds and blossom move to the beat of Krishna's footsteps, once again asserting that Krishna is *svayam kavyam*.

Notice how the *Bhagavata* records his presence in Vrindavana:

> Sometimes Krishna imitated the rapturous notes of the swans
> at other times he danced mimicking dancing peacocks causing his
> companions to laugh. – X.15.11

> With their bodies decorated with tender foliage, peacock feathers
> clusters of flowers and coloured earth

> Balarama and Krishna along with the *gopa*s indulged in dancing,
> wrestling and singing. – X.18.9

> Possessed of a charming personality like an accomplished actor
> graced by a crown of peacock feathers
> his ears decorated by Karnikara flowers
> clad in garments yellow like molten gold
> wearing the Vaijayanti garland made of five different colours
> filling the holes of his flute with the nectar of his lips
> accompanied by the *gopi*s singing his glory
> Krishna entered Vrindavana and beautified it with his footprints.
> – X.21.5

> Picturesquely clad in garments intertwined with tender mango leaves
> with tufts of peacock feathers and bunches of flowers
> and wearing garlands of lilies and lotuses
> and singing and dancing freely in the midst of groups of *gopa*s
> they (Balarama and Krishna) appeared very beautiful like actors
> on the stage. – X.21.8

Jayadeva in the twelfth century broke new ground with his mellifluous *Gita Govinda*. Written in flawless classical Sanskrit Jayadeva created not just beautiful poetry but a love song. The *mangalacharana* of this song where Radha makes her appearance for the first time brings about a paradigm shift in the Shringara Rasa of Krishna poetry. Krishna's romantic liaison is not only

His beloved but becomes His *shakti*, and this paves the way for a more theological interpretation of *shringara* and this would eventually lead to the establishment of Gaudiya Vaishnavaism. However, throughout the *Gita Govinda*, we have numerous beautifully romantic situations where feelings of love intermingle with the fertility and fecundity of the world around and a love song is heard from the bees and the blossoms, the waves of the Yamuna and the conversations of the birds, the rustle of leaves but the source and sustenance of this song is the love of Krishna who by His mere presence transforms everything with His *madhurya*. Jayadeva creates a song of Krishna with sonorous sounds and evocative colours, images of the pleasure of belonging and the poignancy of longing, and in this aesthetically charged atmosphere Krishna becomes a *geet* (song). When Radha and Krishna come together in the end, Radha wishes to become *krishnamaya* not through religious rites and rituals but by Krishna's sensual touch. She says:

Bhagavata Purana, Western India, 16th century, Dehejia Collection of Krishna Art

kuru yadu nandanan chandan

One of the last compositions in Sanskrit was the *Rasamanjari* by Bhanudatta in the fifteenth century. Bhanudatta continued the tradition of romantic Sanskrit poetry and built on the traditional *nayikabheda* (classification of romantic heroines), but went on to provide an elaborate taxonomy, not only of romantic heros and heroines, but of the many and varied romantic situations. The *Rasamanjari* far from being an arid and prosaic document shows a deep poetic awareness and sensitivity of the many moods and seasons, the changing colours and resonances of the mind of the *nayika* and the *nayaka* and which bring into play *sarojasundarachamatkara* (74) (or the wondrous arts of love). The poetry of the *Rasamanjari* leaves no doubt that romantic activity was no idle pastime or a trivial sport but it was a sincere commitment and a lifelong dedication of the romantic persona, who totally believed in their love and defined their lives in its pursuit and fulfilment. To such a person the celebration of romantic love was the *raison d'être* for life and living. This is the central message one derives from the *Rasamanjari*.

Bhanudatta recognizes that romantic exchanges rarely need words but are even more beautifully conveyed by suggestive signs and gestures. The hero desirous of having a romantic rendezvous is asked by the beloved to meet her at sunset:

> When the lover holds in his hand
> the golden lime fruit
> the moon-faced *nayika* puts a dot on the sun that is painted on the wall. – 112

And when Bhanudatta wishes to caution the *nayika* of the possibility of scandal mongers at a tryst, he says:

> My friend you may gladly proceed to the bower to see Krishna
> but be careful of the humming bees hovering there during the day
> and the *chakora*s roaming at night with their garrulous beaks. – 3.15

Equally Bhanudatta uses the facility of Sanskrit in conveying two meanings with one word. For instance in using the word *sneha*, meaning both oil and love:

God created the moon-faced Radha like a flame of light for this earth
As ill luck would have it this flame is dying
Oh Krishna! Refresh this flame with your oil (love)
So that the three worlds are not immersed in darkness.
– 99

Bhanudatta while providing an elaborate taxonomy intersperses his *nayikabheda* with descriptions of beautiful romantic moments, like:

The modest *nayika* is in a dilemma. To fall asleep is to lose sight of the adored one, to remain awake is to risk physical possession. – 9

The *nayika*, lest the morning should bring the love play to a close hastily covers the lotuses in her ears with the hem of her garment so that their opening may not announce the dawn of day. – 10

A king examines paintings, Rajasthan, c.1760, National Museum, Delhi

Oh traveller! the sun being piercingly hot today it is proper for you to rest on the bank of the river adorned with rows of jasmine creepers entwining Tamala trees. – 23

The sweet-eyed *nayika* turned pale like the leaves of a Palmyra tree when she learnt that the clove creepers which grew at her trysting place had shed their leaves with the advent of the month of Chaitra. – 27

The deer-eyed *nayika* adorned herself with flowers and ornaments, scented her curly hair and put betel leaves beside her bed. Her fair body bedecked with gold and *ketaki* flowers lighted up the chamber. – 66

By sweet trickery she puts her mother-in-law to sleep, covers the flame of the lamp and by producing sounds like the cooing of pet doves makes a sign to her lover to come. – 68

The concluding chapter of the *Rasamanjari* is called Darshana in which Bhanudatta describes the various ways in which the beloved is visualized, in a dream, through a picture or in an actual meeting, but for the avid *rasika* the *Rasamanjari*, in providing a vision of the variegated moods and colours of the mind of one who is in love, and the various arts and rituals it inspires, is indeed a *karnabhushanam* (an ornament for their ears).

In the sixteenth century Krishna comes to occupy a different place in Shringara Rasa *kavya*. This was the time of Ritikavya (mannered poetry) which was inaugurated by Keshavdas of Orchha. Keshavdas is a Krishna *bhakta*, notice this verse:

To Him who is the embodiment of love Keshav urges all connoisseurs to pay respect to Him. – 1.2

However, he moves away from the pastoral Vrindavana of the *Bhagavata* and the *Gita Govinda* to the opulence and sophistication of the Rajput courts for that is where Krishna poetry was patronized. Equally he opts for Brajbhasha rather than Sanskrit. Brajbhasha has a musical texture, its consonants are soft and its words have many vowels and this made it the perfect language for romantic poetry. Is it possible that when Kavita was speaking when she was inside Krishna that she spoke in Braj? It has rightly been said that Brajbhasha poets wove a garland of flowers with its words and kept it fragrant with the silken threads of metre and texture. The *shringara* that Keshavdas creates is courtly and not pastoral, its concerns are the many nuances and situations of romantic love at the human level, a love that is earthy and not celestial, it is concerned with matters of the heart and not of the state, it is driven by heart-throbbing emotion and not religious dictates or moralizing ethics. It is worth stressing that Ritikavya is concerned with *lokaranjana* (human pleasure) and not *lokamangala* (human emancipation). However, at the same time even though the *nayaka* and *nayika* are courtly and secular figures, the images of Krishna and Radha are always in the background and the *Rasikapriya* operates at least two levels simultaneously. The beauty and the strength of Ritikavya is that it moves effortlessly and fluidly between the secular and the sacred, from courtly to devotional, from sensuous to spiritual, from Krishna to the courtly *nayaka*, and all this because and through the persona of Krishna, who is now a god and now a human. If the beauty of the *Rasikapriya* is the *nayika* in all her varied moods its strength is the overarching presence of Krishna.

Braj poetry and poetics challenged the hegemony of Sanskrit in pre-colonial India and took an honoured place in the ivory towers of Alamkarashastra and the high priest of Braj rhetoric was Keshavdas, Bihari and Sunder. By the middle of the seventeenth century Brajbhasha had acquired a legitimacy and challenged the dominance of Sanskrit and Braj writers acquired parity with their Sanskrit counterparts. This was particularly true of Shringara Rasa *kavya* like the *Rasikapriya*.

The Rajput courts of central and north-west India saw the heyday of Ritikavya and *khayal bandish*es in Brajbhasha, where under the umbrella of Krishna *bhakti*, *rati shringara* could flourish; at the same time in poetry, dance and music, and all this was to translate into miniature painting in their ateliers. It was Brajbhasha that was to seamlessly bring these arts together and weave them into a tapestry of love.

It was in the court of Kishangarh that a poet and his consort were celebrated as Radha and Krishna. The poet was Savant Singh, whose heart was not in matters of the state but in the romantic episodes of Krishna. He wrote under the pen-name, Nagaridas and his consort, Bani Thani, wrote under the name Rasikbihari. It was the court artist Nihal Chand, who created a portrait of Bani Thani that became so popular that it created a new style.

If the *ritikavi* was a Krishna *bhakta* so was the audience who were the courtiers of the Rajput court. The Rajput psyche was nurtured through martial conflicts, but when he was not at war the Rajput wanted to celebrate his own Vaishnava identity, and this he did by upholding the romantic Krishna through the gem-like words of Ritikavya of the *Rasikapriya*. This assertion was not only through religious rituals but equally by aesthetic rejuvenation through song, dance and painting. As the Rajputs reasserted their dominance both politically and culturally the time for both the grand Sanskrit narrative *mahakavya* (epic poetry), and the Puranas was over, no new monumental temples were built although their influence was very much a part of the culture. Krishna had already been established and valorized as the prototypical romantic hero in the *Bhagavata*, the *Gita Govinda* and by the *ashtachhaapa kavi*s like Surdas, and the time was ripe not for the enjoyment of grand romantic narratives but of romantic moments through the *bhasha*s, in all its rich and varied sensuality and manifold situations, but which was never far removed from an underlying spirituality of the classical Shringara Rasa. Hari *shringara* and *riti shringara* could never be totally separated and in this lies the magic of Krishna, for if Krishna is *shringara* poetry, then the reverse is also true, namely, that wherever there is *shringara* Krishna is not far. The ethos of the time was one of courtly ceremony and not of temple rituals, of sophisticated courtiers and not of rustic cowherds, of urban pleasures and not of pastoral enjoyment, of urbane settings and not idyllic pastures and of a princely Krishna that was valorized through poetry in the *bhasha*s and not the Krishna of the idyllic and bucolic Vrindavana, a bardic and not a Puranic Krishna. It has been rightly said that art in Rajput courts became sweet and tender in the celebration of romantic love, but yet elusive, at once heart piercing and tranquil in its revelation as mystical experience through its in-built metaphors and all this through Ritikavya in Brajbhasha and its paintings in the miniature genre.

Ritikavya celebrates that same romantic love of Krishna of the *Bhagavata* but it now moves fluidly between religious devotion and urbane romanticism, moving seamlessly between *riti* and *bhakti*, and between the court and the *haveli*. The *ritikala* poets richly embraced the romantic love of the courtly Radha and Krishna and north India resonated with their beautiful compositions, and the love of Radha and Krishna took on yet another dimension, another nuance, and the Rajput ateliers hummed with Ritikavya as well as the *Bhagavata* and a new phase of *shringara* poetry and painting was ushered in, a genre which would see Krishna and Radha, as *nayaka*s and *nayika*s in a courtly setting. Krishna had transformed Himself into a courtly nayaka due to His poetic persona.

Bihari Satsai, Datia, 18th century, San Diego Museum of Art

Ritikavya was mannered and stylized, short and fragmentary, and it was richly nuanced and not direct, and was not overtly devotional. Krishna and Radha in Ritikavya were not always referred to directly, neither were romantic sentiments and situations presented literally, and it did not have the devotional veneration and surrender of *bhakti* poetry. In Ritikavya Krishna and Radha were ever present in the background, so that every *nayaka* and *nayika* were reflections of Krishna and Radha, and amorous exchanges and engagements were to be imagined and not presented as such. So strong was the paradigm of the Krishna and Radha as a romantic couple and as protagonists of Shringara Rasa, that every *nayaka* and *nayika* in Ritikavya were in the likeness of Krishna and Radha. *Ritikala* poets were Krishna *bhakta*s but were able to achieve the nuances and shades of Shringara Rasa with well-sculpted and minimal words, through the use of words in Brajbhasha that were both metaphoric and musical, and equally pithy and measured. However in spite of this courtly ambiance of Ritikavya the piety surrounding the persona of Krishna nor the underlying divinity of Krishna, and equally the *paramatman–jivatman* metaphor of the individual atman and the cosmic *atman*, was never lost sight of. Romantic love is all about that beautiful, charged, amorous, intense, albeit transient moment, it is not an elaborate love story. By its very nature romantic moments are evanescent, spontaneous, unexpected and unrehearsed, and it is only the skilled poet or the consummate artist who is able to capture that heart-throbbing moment and convert it into a moment of beauty in an artistic creation. These evanescent romantic moments are complete in themselves, for what they lack in their narrative content they more than make up in their emotional surcharge, for in that momentary and intense romantic happening there is not only the outpouring of the heart but in that poetic moment is the fulfilment of one's very being. The beauty of that moment can only be captured poetically, whether it be through lyrics of the poet or the brush of the artist. That poetic moment of Ritikavya is alive and throbbing, moving and sensuous, in that brief moment there is a whole universe of feeling, it is a still moment within orbits of amorous movements and activities. It is a moment of sheer romantic beauty, be it of longing or rejoicing, of belonging or expectant waiting, of bubbling joy or heart-rending remorse, of anger or jealousy, of the many seasons and faces of romance, all of that and more, fully alive and present in that brief but beautiful poetic moment. It is that brief but beautiful poetic moment which we shall explore in this journey.

Puhakar's Rasabeli, Malwa, 18th century, National Museum, Delhi

When Krishna manifests himself in Ritikavya it is indeed a testament and document of the creative imagination of the poet and the painter and equally the recreation of that emotion by the *rasika* in their celebration of the art and the foundation of this is because *krishnah svayam kavyam*.

Another significant *ritikala* poet whose gem-like verses shine in the repertoire of Ritikavya was Bihari. Born towards the end of the sixteenth century in Orchha and having spent his creative life at Agra and Amber, Bihari's couplets are said to have appeared insignificant but inflicted a deep wound like the arrow of a hunter.

Colours were important to Bihari for they conveyed more than words could speak:

Her pink cheek is so tender
and fragrant
that the rose petal that got
stuck to it
could not be distinguished.

Also:

How perfectly the yellow
Champa garland blends
with your hue dear girl
It can be seen only when its flowers
fade.

And in this invocatory verse Bihari brilliantly uses the language of colours to pay homage to Radha:

Radha take away the pain of existence, the cycle of the world,
from me you whose golden reflection
turns Krishna's blue
complexion into a glowing green.

In other *doha*s Bihari uses words as a painter would use colours and says that the radiance of Radha's limbs makes the white *malati* flowers grow golden, and the crimson streaked eyes are like twilight, the river turns a saffron yellow whenever she plunges into it, her limbs glisten like yellow jasmine, her feet are redder than lacquer dye, her ruby red feet shed dust as a *dhupariya* flower has blossomed at each step and her ravishing eyes are as dark as black bees.

Bihari wrote in Brajbhasha and he colours his words, ornaments his phrases and imparts a certain fragrance to his verses and his *doha*s, brief but elegant, are sheer music to our ears as they weave through every situation and mood of romantic love. His *Satsai* was a landmark in romantic poetry for not only was it copied, translated and commented upon, but it inspired miniature artists to render them into paintings, and it can be said that if Keshavdas' *Rasikapriya* gave painters endless romantic situations, Bihari's *Satsai* provided inspiration for lyrical representations of romantic love.

Of all the human emotions that of romantic love is closely tied to the changing seasons, each month bringing a special message to the beloved, every season a special reminder of the joys of love and longing, the changing seasons reflecting the varying moods of romantic love and the songs of the seasons echoing a melody that resonates through the heart of the lover and the beloved. *Shadrituvarnana* (the description of the six seasons) – Vasanta, Grishma, Varsha, Hemanta, Shravan and Shisira – is an important part of the Kavya literature in Sanskrit. However, Sanskrit literature did not have *barahmasa* poetry. It was Apabhramsha literature, precursor of Hindi, that developed a rich description of the seasons and tied to romantic love. In this genre there is *chaumasa*, poetry which had either four or six seasons or *barahmasa* which was a description of the seasons of the twelve months. The vernacular and oral *barahmasa* later becomes an important part of the literary poetic tradition, both secular as well as Hindu, Jaina and Sufi religious poetry. While religious *barahmasa* remains didactic in nature and were used to impart religious instruction, the village *chaumasa* and *barahmasa* were romantic and were village women's rain songs, especially in north India from

Raga Vasanta, Mewar, c.1750, Philadelphia Museum of Art

Gujarat to Bengal, where they sang of their isolation from their husbands either in the rainy four months from

Ashadha to Ashvin or through the twelve months. These rain songs are based on the sociology of the absent husband, who is away from home either on business or on duty, and the wife either longs for his return in the rainy season or urges him not to leave at all. Seasonal poetry of this genre also was a feature of folk theatre. There was some variation in not only in the number of seasons but in their chronology as well, and one of the poetic conventions was that while Sanskrit *shadritu* poetry described the erotic joys of the lover and the beloved when they are together, the *chaumasa* and *barahmasa* dealt with the *premika*'s longing and fear of separation from her beloved. *Viraha barahmasa* (the seasonal poetry of longing) remains the most evocative in this genre of romantic poetry and in this group the *barahmasa* compositions of Keshavdas who wrote the *Rasikapriya* stand out among others. *Barahmasa* poetry is not only poignant love poetry on the one hand but shows the close resonance between the psyche of the heroine and the mood of the seasons; each season not only possessing a different colour but a distinct message for those in love. In expressing her lament and relating it to the colours and moods of the seasons the heroine equates the throbbing of her heart with the pulsating sap of the trees, the trembling longing within her to the movement of the clouds and the agony of her forlorn state to the pain of lonely birds. Thus she is not alone in her anguish, her piquant cry is heard by the birds and the blossoms that surround her and who understand and share her pain perhaps more than her beloved. In *barahmasa* poetry we see the strong and sympathetic resonance between the romantic mind of the *nayika* and the natural world around her, it is a world that shares her romantic urges and longings, and she defines her love with the same life and energy that animates the trees and the birds and who stand in mute testimony to her love.

Keshavdas in his *barahmasa* converts the lunar calendar into romantic poetry that vividly celebrates the months as it evokes the pain of the *nayika* of the impending separation from her beloved.

Puhakar, a Kashmiri poet, describes Krishna's concern for Radha's delicate feet, in these lines:

After spending the night in Vrindavana
sharing amorous pleasures
and when the moon was about to set
Radha started to walk homewards
Krishna placed lotus leaves
so that her feet would not be hurt by thorns.

The eighteenth century saw another kind of Krishna poet, whose creations were *bija-mantra*s, seeds from which artists created visual images that resonated with *raga*s. Here was a case of poetry and music coming together. These were Ragamala paintings and in the genre of Krishna *shringara* we have Raga Vasanta and Raga Megha Malhar that captured the romantic persona of Krishna as both Vasanta and Varsha are the two seasons that speak to us of Krishna's *shringara*. In both the Ragamalas we see Krishna dancing amidst blossoms and under rain-filled clouds and expressing and sharing *shringara* with everyone around.

An important genre of Shringara Rasa *kavya* is *khayal bandish*es. While Amir Khusro (1253–1325) is considered the father of *khayal bandish*, it was during the Vaishnava *bhakti* movement that *bandish* in Brajbhasha based on Krishna *shringara* became an integral part of classical Hindustani music. It was in the court of the Mughal emperor Muhammad Shah Rangila (1702-48) that Niyamat Khan (Sadarang) and his nephew Firoz Khan (Adarang) popularized *khayal bandish*. Within the well-sculpted words of *khayal bandish* one almost hears the hushed voices of Krishna and the *gopi*s and these little jewels of poetry travelled orally across centuries from village to temple and palace to proscenium and *khayal* almost become synonymous with Krishna *shringara*.

Veneration of Shrinathji, painting on wood by Trilok Soni

So Krishna is indeed both the *kavi* and the *kavya*, the *rasa* and the *rasika*, the *shabda* and the *artha*; He is *Purusha* and *Prakriti*. Who then are we, who are *rasika*s of Krishna *shringara*? We celebrate Shringara Rasa *kavya*, its forms and textures, its sounds and rhythms, its colours and melodies, its music and metaphors. Krishna dances and frolics, speaks and sings, and *shringara* in its many colours comes alive for us through *kavya*; we are the *gopi*s and the *gopa*s of Vrindavana, the *nayaka*s and the *nayika*s of Ritikavya. But this is not the finale of our aesthetic experience of Krishna. *Sakar* Krishna must become the *nirakar* Krishna once again and this can only happen when the form of Krishna dissolves into the many visions of Krishna in everything around us, when we can say that when we experience *madhurya* anywhere we experience Krishna. That *madhurya* will come to us from the joyous togetherness of a *premi* and a *premika*, the evocative sight of a *pranaya mandapa*, a pair of birds sitting on a branch, a *lata* winding around a tree trunk, a bee hovering from flower to flower, a peacock dancing at the sight of rain clouds, lotuses blooming and opening their petals to the sun. All love is that of Krishna, the hushed words of romance between a man and a woman are those of Krishna and Radha, all poetry that celebrates romantic love is that of Krishna so that we can turn the sentence around and say *kavyam svayam krishnam.*

When our journey of the poets and painters who have made Krishna *shringara* alive through their creations comes to an end, we begin to understand how Krishna becomes *svayam kavyam*, how the *kavi* and the *kavya* are no longer *dvaita* but *advaita*, not two but one like Krishna and Radha and when we are in the beautiful and majestic realm of Krishna's *shuddha advaita*, colours and sounds, movement and touch, aroma and taste, all speak to us of Krishna's *shringara* and all of a sudden we realize that if Krishna is *shringara*, *shringara* is also Krishna, and the world outside and the mind inside become *krishnamaya.*

The romantic Krishna finds a textual basis for the first time in the tenth book of the ninth-century *Bhagavata Purana* and then for a thousand years the *shringara* of Krishna is celebrated in poetry both in Sanskrit and the *bhasha*s by poets and painters. While in the *Bhagavata* Krishna dallies amorously with the *gopi*s, it is in the twelfth-century *Gita Govinda* that Jayadeva introduces Radha as Krishna's romantic partner. Following this Chaitanya in the fourteenth century makes Radha as Krishna's consort and she is considered a *devi.* We have bypassed Chaitanya in our journey as he converted the *jugalajodi* of Radha and Krishna to that of a god and a goddess. However, nowhere is there any mention of a marriage between Krishna and the *gopi*s or Radha. Anytime a man and a woman are romantically involved it is very common to question whether they are married to each other or whether they are married to someone else and if this is an adulterous relationship. Questions like this are most inappropriate when it comes to Krishna and *gopi*s or Radha as they are not historical persons and do not answer to social, moral and legal questions about their relationships. To ask such questions is to betray ignorance about our Puranas, their language and purpose, their myths and metaphors. The *Bhagavata Purana* is not a historical narrative of Krishna and to raise questions about the propriety of Krishna's romantic relationships is to desecrate the beauty and sacrality of the *dashama skandha* where Krishna and the *gopi*s are wrapped in the folds of *madhura bhava* or a loving and sweet togetherness in the enchanted Vrindavana. This togetherness, nay a dance, is not just of a man and a woman but of *Purusha*, the macrocosmic reality with *Prakriti*, the microcosmic reality; it is the coming together of the divine with the human, of the sky with the earth. This is preceded in the Purana by Krishna's cosmic acts even as a child so we should be prepared to also read His amorous acts mythically. If we are comfortable with Krishna as Damodara or the child who is tied to a mortar and who then upturns it, why do we see Krishna as a mere mortal when he is with the *gopi*s and Radha? Krishna is divine and human at the same time and Krishna's involvement with the *gopi*s and later with Radha, is the coming together of *Purusha* and *Prakriti* in a joyous abandon in the mythic Vrindavana, which is no ordinary forest but the metaphor of our inner mind (*atman*) where *madhura dhara* (streams of honey flow). If Krishna, Radha and Vrindavana are all mythic representations, should it not behoove us to understand them and their relationship through the lens of a myth rather than the parameters of history or rational human behaviour? Need we ask how old is Radha and whether she is a married woman? Need we question whether Krishna's behaviour is unworthy or immoral? Krishna seeks Radha even as she longs for Him and together they find bliss by being together in the serenity of the *nikunja* (the secret groves of Vrindavana). It is in that grove that we have to find Krishna, not with our rational mind but with a mind that is chastened with the sound of the flute and which has moved away from the outer and superficial mental stirring to the depths

Krishna in Vrindavana, painting by Girish Patel

of the inner and serene mind devoid of *chitta vritti*. In that beautiful space in the mind, as in the groves of Vrindavana where Krishna dallies, there are no worldly questions, no raised eyebrows or the pointing of fingers when a man and a woman come together, but just the celebration of the romance of *Purusha* and *Prakriti* (a union of the sky and the earth) a state of *atmarati, atmanistha* and *atmadarshana*, an *atman* that is rich with the presence of both *Purusha* and *Prakriti*. This is the true meaning of the romance of Krishna and the *gopi*s and Radha, for they are one, it is only we who see them as two. The Krishna and Radha relationship is not a historical or fictional narrative but a Puranic account, a mythic trope, to reflect poetic truth.

Barahmasa, Varsha Ritu, painting in Kangra style by Vijay Sharma

कृष्ण काव्य

Krishna Poetry

The genesis of poetry is often unknown and mysterious, yet many are the reasons for why poetry is created. For Valmiki it is *shoka* (deep-seated grief) that led to *shloka* (poetry). Krishna poetry generally arises from a desire to celebrate the many-splendoured persona of Krishna, His heart-warming *krida* and His awe-inspiring *leela*. A poet once said: "I do not know why poets write poetry, but for me it is only an excuse to remember the love of Radha and Krishna." For Krishna poets, it is the mere thought of Krishna that is transformed into poetry, words of His beautiful form arise in the mind and quickly become evocative, at the mere thought of Krishna the words begin to dance, when the colour *ghanashyama* comes to mind it is as if the words are drenched with *rasa*, when the *pitambara* flutters in the mind's eye as He dances the words acquire a rhythm and when finally when the sound of the flute is heard the words become a song and begin to move. And once Krishna poetry is formed, a poet like Bihari will ask that the image of Krishna thus created never leave his mind, another poet likes it to a fragrant flower as its aroma spreads and *rasika*s gather around it like bees to the lotus, or another poet like Bhanudatta will ensure that it becomes a *karnaphula* (an ornament for the ear) for ever adorning those of us who adore Krishna. The mere words of Krishna poetry as Bihari says are stronger than arrows, for they may appear small but they pierce the heart. And when Krishna poetry is sung aloud in front of the cognoscenti it is transformed into a dance and painters are inspired to dip their *kalam* into their paint and create a Krishna painting. Thus the mere thought of Krishna is a poem, His mere remembrance is a song, and when the mind is rapturous with His presence words become flowers with which we adorn His feet. And when these flowers fade we take them as *nirmalya* and hold them in our hands as we become totally *krishnamaya*.

Painting in western Indian style by Vijay Sharma

Bilvamangala
Probably from Karnataka in the eighth century wrote a seminal work, *Balagopalastuti*, eulogizing the child Krishna.

Bilvamangala

You have been decorated with a *tilaka* of *kasturi*
on Your forehead
with the *kaustubha* ornament on Your chest
the *navamaulikam* on Your nose
a flute in Your hands
and a bracelet on Your wrist
Your body bedecked with fragrant sandalwood paste
with the *muktavali* around Your neck
You liberate the *gopi*s who played the *rasaleela* with You
Victory to You Gopala, You are the crest jewel.

Painting in Chaurapanchashika style by Devendra Sharma

Bilhana
He was a eleventh-century poet from Kashmir who wrote the haunting poem *Chaurapanchashika* describing his love for Champa.

Bilhana

I have still to decide whether
she is Parvati or Urvashi or Lakshmi.
Or was she created by Brahma
to make the world mad?
Or was it that the Lord Himself
wanted to see this jewel among women?

Painting in Kangra style by Vijay Sharma

Bhagavata Kavi
It was in the ninth-century Pandya country of Tamil Nadu
that inspired brahmins composed the *Bhagavata Purana* and made Shukdev the narrator.

Bhagavata Purana

Sometimes Krishna imitated the
rapturous notes of the swans
at other times he danced mimicking dancing
peacocks causing his companions to laugh.
– X.15.11

With their bodies decorated
with tender foliage, peacock feathers
clusters of flowers and coloured earth
Balarama and Krishna along with the *gopa*s
indulged in dancing, wrestling and singing.
– X.18.9

Painting in Kullu style by Vijay Sharma

Bhagavata Kavi
It was in the ninth-century Pandya country of Tamil Nadu that inspired brahmins composed the *Bhagavata Purana* and made Shukdev the narrator.

Bhagavata Purana

Possessed of a charming personality like an
accomplished actor
graced by a crown of peacock feathers
his ears decorated by Karnikara flowers
clad in garments yellow like molten gold
wearing the Vaijayanti garland
made of five different colours
filling the holes of His flute
with the nectar of His lips
accompanied by the *gopi*s singing His glory
Krishna entered Vrindavana
and beautified it with His footprints.
– X.21.5

Painting in Kullu style by Vijay Sharma

Bhagavata Kavi
It was in the ninth-century Pandya country of Tamil Nadu that inspired brahmins composed the *Bhagavata Purana* and made Shukdev the narrator.

Bhagavata Purana

Picturesquely clad in garments intertwined
with tender mango leaves
with tufts of peacock feathers and bunches of flowers
and wearing garlands of lilies and lotuses
and singing and dancing freely in the
midst of groups of *gopa*s
they (Balarama and Krishna) appeared very beautiful
like actors on the stage.

– X.21.8

Painting in Kangra style by Vijay Sharma

Jayadeva

He was a twelfth-century poet of Odisha who wrote the immortal classic, the *Gita Govinda*.

Jayadeva

She is richly arrayed in ornaments for the battle of love
tangles of flowers lie wilted in her loosened hair
she is visibly excited by embracing Hari
her necklaces tremble on full hard breasts
curling locks caress her moon face
she is weary from ardently kissing His lips
drops of sweat wet the graceful body
fallen limp on His chest in passionate battle.

– *Gita Govinda* 7

Pichhwai by Trilok Soni.

Ashtachhaapa Kavis

Of all the Krishna poets, the *ashtachhaapa kavi*s are unique. Dedicated to Krishna as Shrinathji they were inducted initially by Vallabhacharya and then by Vitthalnathji in the service of Krishna. The eight poets were allotted the *ashtapraharas* (the eight watches of the day) and sitting in the *nija griha* (the sanctum) their voices resonated in the entire *haveli* and the congregation joined them. Surdas was the foremost of the eight and he recreated the *leela*s and *krida*s of Krishna from the *dashama skandha* and created many new situations of the amorous sports of Krishna like the *danaleela*. The initial songs of Surdas were inspired by Vallabhacharya but in his later songs we see the distinct influence of Vitthaldas. Singing in Brajbhasha Surdas created a unique type of poetry where the young Krishna comes alive and He does not remain a distant deity but becomes a cherished friend. His songs spread all over the Hindi belt and especially in Mewar where Rajasthani artists created evocative paintings and *pichhwai*s.

Madhurashtakam
Picchwai by Trilok Soni.

Madhurashtakam

Mahaprabhu Vallabhacharya's *Madhurashtakam* is fundamental to the understanding of the *shringara* of Krishna in the *Bhagavata*. *Madhurya* (honey like sweetness) has both epistemologic and ontologic value, in other words it not only gives us the expressions but equally the experience of Krishna and becomes the foundation of the *shuddha advaita* of the *Bhagavata*. Our *atman*, according to the *Bhagavata*, has *madhura dhara* (streams of honey) which Krishna activates with His *shringara*. This has another philosophic suggestion and, that is, *madhurya* is frozen in our *atman* and Krishna only activates it; that is, we remember what is forgotten our love for Krishna is ancient. Krishna is *akhilam madhuram* (altogether sweet); but that is not enough for He ensures that by His very *sannidhya* (presence) everything around Him is also sweet. This includes all of Vrindavana, the birds and the blossoms, the *gopa*s and the *gopi*s.

Painting in Mewar style by Savant Singh Naruka

Surdas (1478–1563)
Foremost of the *ashtachhaapa kavis* was inducted by Vallabhacharya and is a poet of the Pushtimarga Sampradaya that celebrates Krishna as Shrinathji.

Surdas

See, here comes the son of Nanda,
as He is called in Vrindavana.
Having lotus-like eyes, He plays upon a flute,
which is Yashoda's delight.
He addresses the cows by their names
as Kari, Gori, Dhori and Dhumar.
Together with His friends, the *gopa*s,
He takes delight in drinking milk.
Surdas aspires that Krishna
may bestow kindness upon him.

Painting in Basohli style by Vijay Sharma

Vidyapati (1352–1448)
He was the court poet of Shivasimha of Mithila and wrote in Maithili and it is said that he, more than any other poet, understood the mind of the *nayika*.

Vidyapati

As mirror to my hand, flowers to my hair
kajal to my eyes, *tambula* to my mouth
musk to my breast, necklace to my neck
ecstasy to my flesh, heart to my home
as wings to a bird, water to fish
life to the living, so you are to me.
But tell me, Madhava beloved
who are you, who are you really?

Painting in Kangra style by Vijay Sharma

Gang
He was part of the atelier of Akbar and wrote evocative Krishna poetry.

Gang

On one side, a *sakhi* waves a fan
on the other side, a *sakhi* holds a box of betel
from behind another *sakhi* gives her the betel leaf
and when Radha opens her mouth
the scarlet of her lips flashes out
just at that moment
the son of Nanda played His flute
and there came upon them
the remembrance of the bowers
and then they all swooned and fell on the ground.

Painting in Basohli style by Vijay Sharma

Rasakhan (1548–1628)
Born in Amroha (present-day Uttar Pradesh) of Afghan parents, Rasakhan is considered a Muslim Vaishnava.

Rasakhan

Rasakhan says:

I searched for Brahma
in the ancient songs of *Samaveda* and
the hymns of the *Rigveda* with great enthusiasm.

But yet I could neither see His form
nor learn of His true nature.

Calling out His name I searched for Him everywhere
but nobody could help me.

Just then I found Him touching
the feet of Radha in a bower.

Painting in Basohli style by Vijay Sharma

Rasakhan (1548–1628)
Born in Amroha (present-day Uttar Pradesh) to Afghan parents, Rasakhan is considered a Muslim Vaishnava.

Rasakhan

With your wealth you may intimidate Kubera
with your beauty you may defy Kamadeva
Having unlimited pleasures you may exceed Indra
and through *yoga* you may
hold the Ganga on your head.
What use of all this, Rasakhan
even if you relish the rapture
of beatitude on your tongue
if wholeheartedly you are not
dyed in the colour of Him
who remains dyed in the colour of Radha?

Painting in Basohli style by Vijay Sharma

Narsinh Mehta,1408-1465 is the adi kavi of Gujarat.

Narsinh Mehta

Sages and *rishi*s are infatuated with your body marks
your beauty is beyond our comprehension
all we see in it is the *maya* of God.
Your ankle bells sing and throb,
the bells tinkle in your hair ornament
your head ornament sparkles like lightning in the sky
your forehead sports the saffron mark
and the *tilaka* of musk
your eyes are like petals, your gait is coquettish
where did you have your *choli* stitched?
And who taught you how to cover your head?
And who did your braid?
The maidens of Braj are infatuated
and they look in all directions with restless eyes
as if to spread the message of Madan.
Look at the beautiful maiden for in her
is the presence of Mohini.

Painting in Kishangarh style by Hukam Chand

Narsinh Mehta, 1408-1465 is the adi kavi of Gujarat.

Narsinh Mehta

Awake Yashoda's life, it is dawn
under your pillow are my clothes
just turn and I will pull away my *odhani*
and go with my *sakhi*s to fetch water.
The birds are singing my beloved
and the night is about to end.
Get up from your bed and give up your indolence
if I wake you up with my voice
then the neighbours will hear
if I twist your toe your anklets will sound.
One becomes what one thinks
unless Narsinh's lord wakes up, the day will not
begin.

Painting in Kishangarh style by Hukam Singh

Savant Singh in the 18th century was the ruler of Kishangarh and Bani Thani was his consort. They were both poets.

Savant Singh

There are only two places a flower can rest –
At the feet of Krishna
And on your
beautiful hair.

Painting in Basohli style by Vijay Sharma

Bhanudatta

He, probably of Kashmiri descent in the fifteenth century, was one of the last of the great Sanskrit poets and in his *Rasamanjari*, he establishes the basis of *nayikabheda*.

Bhanudatta

Radha's eyes were filled with tears
(with remorse at Krishna not having kept the tryst
when she saw Krishna wearing mango blossoms
in His ears and His cheeks yellow with pollen.

Painting in Basohli style by Vijay Sharma

Bhanudatta

He, probably of Kashmiri descent in the fifteenth century, was one of the last of the great Sanskrit poets and in his *Rasamanjari*, he establishes the basis of *nayikabheda*.

Bhanudatta

Oh my mind!

Give up your playfulness.

Oh my friend-like bashfulness!

Pray do not afflict me.

Oh my brotherly eyelids!

Let my eyes open wide.

Oh Kamadeva!

Forgive me for a moment.

The comely Krishna, wearing a peacock feather
on His forehead and blue lotuses in His ears and
carrying a flute in His hands
appears before my eyes.

Painting in Kangra style by Vijay Sharma

Keshavdas (1555–1617)
He is considered the father of Ritikavya. He was the court poet of Indrajit of Orchha and the *guru* of Rai Parveen.

Keshavdas, Rasikapriya

A manifest *dakshina nayaka.*

Oh *Sakhi* !

Krishna's gaze towards me is full of love
and He is still fearful of me.
His speech is as soft as before
and I am still very fond of Him.
He has lost none of virtues and
He is still full of joy and laughter.
I do not have to enumerate all His qualities.
I do not believe you when you say that He
is under the influence of other women.

Painting in Kangra style by Mukesh Dhiman

Keshavdas (1555–1617)
He is considered the father of Ritikavya. He was the court poet of Indrajit of Orchha and the *guru* of Rai Parveen.

Keshavdas, Kavipriya

Lovely creepers are in bloom,
blossoming trees are young once more
and streams and lakes are full of flowers
Women, aglow with passion, dressed in their best
abandon themselves to the sports of love.
The parrot, the *maina*
and the *koyal* are singing songs of love.
Why think of going away, why spoil this joy
in the month of Chaitra, my love?

Painting in Kangra style by Vijay Sharma

Sunder

He was the court poet of Shah Jahan. His main work *Sunder Shringara* was written in 1688.

Sunder

Why do you
worry? said the *sakhi* –
Your face is more beautiful than the moon –
Your body more sensuous than Rati –
He will surely return to you –
Where can He find a person like you?

Painting in Mewar style by Hukam Chand

Bihari

Born towards the end of the sixteenth century in Orchha, Bihari spent his creative life at Agra and then finally at Amber.

Bihari

She has a glow on her face
that every night is like a full-moon night
in this household.
People come to know of the dates
only by referring to the almanac.

Painting in Mewar style by Vijay Sharma

Bihari

Born towards the end of the sixteenth century in Orchha, Bihari spent his creative life at Agra andthen finally at Amber.

Bihari

Dear Radha!

As Krishna puts the flute of green bamboo
to His lips, and the lustre of His red lips, dark eyes
and yellow upper wrap falls on it,
it turns as if dyed in all the colours of the rainbow.

Painting in Odisha style by Bibhu Maharana

Banmali Das was an 18th century poet of Odisha.

Banmali Das

When Radha–Krishna played Holi in great ecstasy
someone sang a eulogy for Him in Raga Basanta
dancing madly and playing the *mridangam*.
They have mixed sandalwood paste and *ittar*
and flocks of *gopi*s play Holi with the son of Nanda.
Someone pretends and snatches away the flute
Someone else pours coloured water
Helpless Krishna runs to catch them.

Painting in Basohli style by Vijay Sharma

Banmali Das was an 18th century poet from Odisha who wrote moving Krishna poetry.

Banmali Das

Shyam entered my room dressed as a woman
on the pretext of painting my feet with *alta*.
Instead He wrote His name on my feet
and put me to shame.

Painting in Kangra style by Vijay Sharma

Raga Tilang.

Khayal Bandish

Shyam charms the mind
and is playful and artful.
I have become smitten
by His picture.
The *gopi*s listen to the melodies of His flute
and this causes love to arise in them.
Such a dancer
and lifter of the mountain
has established Himself
in my mind.

Painting in Mewar style by Vijay Sharma

Raga Puriya

Khayal Bandish

Oh the dark-coloured beloved!
Show me your face
I can only think of you
you have a beautiful face
your eyes are artful
and your gait is enchanting.
Come, let me embrace you.
I cannot accept anything less.

Painting in Kangra style by Vijay Sharma

Raga Des

Khayal Bandish

Oh Shyam of Braj!
You wear Radha's clothes
and dance with me
and all the *sakhi*s.

Painting in Basohli style by Vijay Sharma

Raga Khamaj

Khayal Bandish

Oh *Sakhi* !
One who wears a crown of peacock feathers
has earrings and has placed the flute on His lips
that handsome man is Giridhar Gopal.
His very smile is enough to captivate you.
You lose control of your body and mind.
The women of Braj have become
intoxicated with His looks
and think of Him every minute of day and night.

Painting in Kangra style by Vijay Sharma

Khayal Bandish

Oh Hari!
I have adorned myself.
Love surges in my heart.
With your hand
apply a *tilaka* on my forehead
only then will my adornment be complete.

Painting in Chaurapanchashika style by Devendra Sharma

Raga Kirwani

Khayal Bandish

Oh Nandalal of Braj!
I am uneasy without you.
I beseech you
and place a garland on you
and touch your feet.
I have searched you
all over Vrindavana,
the flute player
who was born in Mathura
and raised in Gokul.

Painting in Kangra style by Vijay Sharma

Raga Hindola

Ragamala

Enjoying the pleasure of being rocked
in the swing by beautiful damsels.
Lustrous grey like the throat of pigeons
is the one described as Hindola Raga
by the best of sages.

Painting in Basohli style by Vijay Sharma

Dharam Vir (1926-97)
He was a renowned Hindi poet, author, playwright and a social thinker.
He was the chief editor of the Hindi weekly *Dharmayug*.

Dharam Vir Bharati

When you sent me folded lotuses
I knew you wanted to meet me at dusk
When you sent me a basket of *bel* flowers
I knew that your fingers longed for me
When you sent me two *agatsya* flowers
I knew that you wanted to meet me
under the shade of a tree by the side of the lake
to paint my toes.

Painting in Basohli style by Vijay Sharma

Unknown Poet

Forgotten Poets

A *nayaka* asked the *nayika*
Who will inherit our love, a love that is so pure?
Touching the earth the *nayika* said
it is the earth that will inherit our love
from it will arise a Kalpavriksha
and on it will sit birds who will sing a song of our love
and when the wind blows through it
it will whisper softly of our romance
and when lovers sit underneath it
they will speak in hushed voices of our love
and when rain falls on the tree
it will gently bring with it our blessings
that all love should be as pure and everlasting as ours.

Painting in Kangra style by Vijay Sharma

Unknown Poet

Seven *gopi*s were going to fetch water
and they seemed like seven musical notes
and when they heard the flute of Krishna
they mingled with the clouds and when it rained
there were notes of Raga Megha Malhar.

Painting in Basohli style by Vijay Sharma

Unknown Poet

When after an amorous night
the morning sun appeared
The *nayaka* left leaving the *nayika* by herself
she felt forsaken and lonely and looked
two pigeons were sporting near the lotus pond.
She dipped her hand in sandalwood paste
and camphor and applied it to a pigeon
and coloured it yellow.
The male not recognizing it any more
flew away leaving the *nayika*
and the yellow pigeon to share their loneliness.

Painting in Kangra style by Vijay Sharma

Nevaj

He was a court poet of Ajam Khān who was a contemporary of Farrukhshiyar.

Nevaj

A *viyogini nayika* cautions her friends
about the ill effects of the sound of the flute.
Do not listen to the sounds of the flute
or else you will be wounded by
the arrows of Kama and fall in love.
The flute is filled with poison
and it spreads this poison in your heart.
Do not get intoxicated with the sweet sounds of
this flute for its effects are dangerous.
You will soon lose your consciousness.
If you care for the honour of your family
close your ears with your fingers.

Painting in Kishangarh style by Hukam Chand

Shambhunath Mishra
He spent his early years in the eighteenth century under the patronage of Bhagvatrai Khinchi.

Shambhunath Mishra

The poet describes a love game of Krishna.
A *nayika* took Krishna in disguise as her
student to Vrishbhanu's home
where a number of ladies had gathered.
The *sakhi*s understood the game
and forced Krishna to touch Radha's feet.
Radha embraced Him and applied a *tilaka* on His head
and said lovingly. Take Him to a lonely spot and
chant *mantra*s and this will make you the head of Braj.

Painting in Kangra style by Vijay Sharma

Mandan
He lived in Jaitpur in Bundelkhand and wrote invocatory verses for Abdurrahim Khankhana.

Mandan

A *nayika* talks to her *sakhi*
about the time she spent with Krishna.
I had gone to the Yamuna to fetch water but on
account of a turn of events
I got into trouble.
Just as I put the pot of water on my head
dark clouds gathered and I was frightened.
In this state my foot got sprained
and I could not climb the steps.
Nanda's youthful son held my hand and lifted me.
May He live long.

Painting in Kishangarh style by Hukam Chand

Unknown Poet

Forgotten Poets

One *sakhi* asked another
I have heard but not known
about Krishna's *madhurya*
Where does He stay and how do I get to see Him?
The *sakhi* replied
Where the Kadamba tree sings a song of love
Where the Parijata whispers
the rhythms of love poetry
Where the wind carries a sweet melody
Where every tree becomes a Kalpavriksha
and every cow a Surabhi
Where the dance of the peacock
and the whisper of the bees
the songs of the birds
and the message of the Yamuna
teaches you a lesson of sweet love
there you will hear the sound of the flute
and it is there that you will meet Krishna.

Painting in Basohli style by Vijay Sharma

Unknown Poet

Radha asked:
Night and day I have worshipped the *devi*
with appropriate rituals
and have loved Krishna.
But why has Krishna not performed
any sacraments of love?

Krishna replied:
The fragrance of the Parijata
and the whispers of the leaves of the Kadamba tree
the rhythms of love in the dance of the peacock
the sweet talk of the bees
and the songs of love in the rain.
Didn't you feel the sacraments of love in them?

Painting in Kangra style by Vijay Sharma

Unknown Poet

The *sakhi*s were jealous of Krishna's attention
towards Radha and gave her a glass of hot milk.
This scalded Radha's throat but she did not complain
as she was lost in thoughts of Krishna.
When Krishna arrived the next day
He had red spots all over His body.

Painting in Basohli style by Vijay Sharma

Unknown Poet

Forgotten Poets

It was a spiritual moment in Vrindavana
and a *gopi* asked another *gopi*
During the day my love is like a bird
its home is in the vast and boundless sky
but as twilight comes it needs a home to rest
it requires an *asana* where it can find comfort.
So they went to Krishna with their question.

Krishna said:
A king sits on a throne for it is the symbol of power
but love needs no power nor glory
it is tender and soft, it should rest on a *padmasana*.
For in the *padma* there is a message
that love should be rooted in *dharati*
but spread in every direction to seek
the radiance of the sun
and the light of the moon.

Painting in Basohli style by Vijay Sharma

Unknown Poet

A *virahini nayika* stood holding the branch of a tree
as a *lata* would around the trunk
two pigeons sported underneath
and two parrots on the branch above
whispered to each other
and peacocks performed a dance of love.
Her *sakhi* asked:
why do you stand thus?

Said the *nayika:*
The pleasures of love are for all to see
the pain of love is only for those who know.
As she said this
a leaf fell from the tree into her *odhani*
and she felt blessed.

Created by the woman of Chamba, Himachal Pradesh.

Forgotten Poets

Many have sat under the Kadamba tree and have partaken of its *chhatra-chhaya*, and as the wind blew through it they have heard the strains of Raga Megha Malhar and when its leaves flutter they begin to hear Raga Hindola, the many voices of Krishna poets, ancient and modern, visit their mind and they are no longer alone. But then the mind yearns for the sight of Krishna, His smile and His flute, His dancing steps and His lotus eyes, and then just as we give up the possibility of finding Him and whisper, *kaun gali gayo shyam* something moves in the branches above us and we see Krishna playing the flute. He teases us and hides from us, makes us search and trace His footsteps, we ask the trees and talk to the birds if they have seen Him, but to the Krishna *shringara bhakta* He is never far as long as He sits under the Kadamba tree they will always find Him.

Pichhwai by Trilok Soni

A fundamental tenet of Vaishnavism is that the world is the body of God, that the infinite is made up of many finites, that *jivatma* is part of *paramatma*. Ramanujacharya was an ardent supporter of this view which came to be called Vishishtadvaita. One of the manifestations of Vishnu is the *virat svarupa* where He contains the entire *samsara* and the cosmos within His body. The *Gita* uses this trope when Krishna wants to exhort Arjuna to action. In the *Gita*, Krishna is the *sarathi* for Arjuna, however our Krishna is the *adi kavi* who contains within his Shringara Kavya the many and multiple *nayika*s of Shringara Rasa. While in the *Bhagavata* it were the *gopi*s and in the *Gita Govinda* there was Radha, for Bhanudatta in the *Rasamanjari* there were manifold *nayika*s and then Keshavdas in his *Rasikapriya* widens the taxonomy of *nayika*s. In the pleasures of belonging or the pathos of longing the *nayika* is multichromatic and expresses a variety of emotions, for after all she is the most beautiful expression of *prakriti*, she is the foundational matter, she is the primal mind of the beloved who with her gestures and eyes and not so much with words expresses the state of her mind. Krishna's *vishala svarupa* pulsates with the many voices and feelings of the *nayika*.

Contemporary Pichhwai

Tribal Poetry from Gujarat

Come to the forest where the flowers are fragrant
We will drink the lotus honey
and make a bed of lotus leaves
Come to the forest where the flowers are fragrant
Leave your pot besides the river
and follow your heart
Come to the forest where the flowers are fragrant
I will play the flute on a moonlit night
Come to the forest where the flowers are fragrant
We will sit under the Kadamba tree
and I will put flowers in your hair
Come to the forest where the flowers are fragrant
I am Kanha and you are Rai,
we will dance till the moon sets
Come to the forest where the flowers are fragrant.

Painting in Kangra style by Vijay Sharma

Radha-Krishna

When our journey of the poets and painters who have made Krishna *shringara* alive through their creations comes to an end, we begin to understand how Krishna becomes *svayam kavyam*, how the *kavi* and the *kavya* are no longer *dvaita* but *advaita*, not two but one, like Krishna and Radha and when we are in the beautiful and majestic realm of Krishna's *shuddha advaita*, colours and sounds, movement and touch, aroma and taste, all speak to us of Krishna's *shringara* and all of a sudden we realize that if Krishna is *shringara*, *shringara* is also Krishna, and the world outside and the mind inside become *krishnamaya*.

Painting in Kangra style by Vijay Sharma

Vidai, as We Take Your Leave

As we leave Krishna's enchanted presence, soaked in His *shringara*, coloured by *ghanashyama*, our entire being touched by His love, we are not ready to be without Him. We are like the *gopi*s at the end of the *maharasa*. There are pangs of *viraha*, the pathos of being separated, the poignancy of being alone in this world without having Him besides us. His sweet smile, the rhythms of His dance and above all the music of His flute seem to have been silenced. But yet we were wrong. Having experienced Krishna's *shringara*, the world if we deeply understand it, is pervaded by Krishna's *madhurya*. Whether it is the limpid waters of the Yamuna, the soft fragrance of the blossoms, the dance of the peacock at the approaching rains, the wind that blows through the Kadamba tree which brings the words of the *Bhagavata*, the rain-filled clouds in the sky which remind us of *ghanashyama* and which bring to us the strains of Raga Megha Malhar and the sweet whisper of the birds who sing the *Madhurashtakam* all bring to us the sounds of His flute. Suddenly Krishna is everywhere, the whole world is *krishnamaya* and we are not alone, but only if we have the transfiguring eyes of love.

Vijay Sharma

If there is a living person who brings together the art and the music, the history and the colours of the Himalayas it must be Vijay Sharma. Vijay's paintings takes us back to the hoary days of Pahari painting and reminds us of the *kalam* of artists like Devidas of Basohli, Nainsukh and Manku, and makes us wonder, is not he a descendant of one of them or any celebrated Pahari artists of the court of yore! There is in his *kalam* refinement and lyricism, in his colours a living emotion, in his compositions an evocative drama. Vijay is skilled in all the styles of Pahari painting which include Kangra, Guler, Chamba, Mankot, but above all he is a master of the Basohli *kalam*. He knows and reads the Takri script. Vijay is largely self-taught but he is quick to point out that he stands on the shoulders of the masters that have come before him. He is especially indebted to the late Shri Vishwanath Ohri of Shimla and the artist late Vedpal Sharma "Bannu" of Rajasthan. Vijay is widely travelled in India and abroad and has an encyclopaedic knowledge of Pahari paintings in the world. He is not only an artist but an art critic, art historian, editor and a prolific writer as well and has lectured in many museums of India and abroad.

He has several articles in prestigious art journals like *MARG* and has authored many books, among them are:

Temple of Devikothi (with Eberhard Fischer and V.C. Ohri); *Chamba Painting: Origin and Development; Love for Pleasure* (with Ludwig V. Habighorst and Peter A. Reichart); *Vision of an Enlightened King;* and *Kangra ki Chitrakan Parampara* (in Hindi

He has received many awards which include:

National Award of Master Craftsman in Basohli Painting in 1990 from the Ministry of Textiles, the AIFACS Award by the All India Fine Arts and Crafts Society in 1997 and the National Kalidas Award in 2011 by the Government of Madhya Pradesh. In 2012 the Government of India bestowed on him Padma Shri and later that year he was awarded the Honorary Doctorate by the Himachal University.

He has trained many junior artists and guided scholars. His opinion is sought by auction houses abroad and his paintings are in many private collections and museums. Vijay's heart is in Pahari paintings and he is one of the greatest living ambassadors of this art form.

I am a *rasika*
with a silent *kalam*
waiting for You to touch it
and make it fragrant with words
and colourful with music
and alive with movement
so that when I remember You
I can compose *kavya*
and offer it to You, Krishna.
It is You, Krishna
who are both the *kavi* and the *kavya*
I am not a *kavi* but it is Your
kavya that makes me who I am,
a Krishna *rasika*.